Contents

Rigby
A Harcourt Achieve Imprint

www.Rigby.com
1-800-531-5015

What is the National Park Service?

The National Park Service began in 1916 and is a group that is in charge of caring for all national park areas in the United States. Over time the service also began caring for seashores, battle sites, and historic buildings, like the Lincoln Memorial in Washington, D.C. Big or small, natural or man-made, living or nonliving, the National Park System works hard to protect the treasured places in the United States so these special places will not disappear.

All National Park Service areas have this symbol on their signs.

NATIONAL
PARK
SERVICE

Department
of the Interior

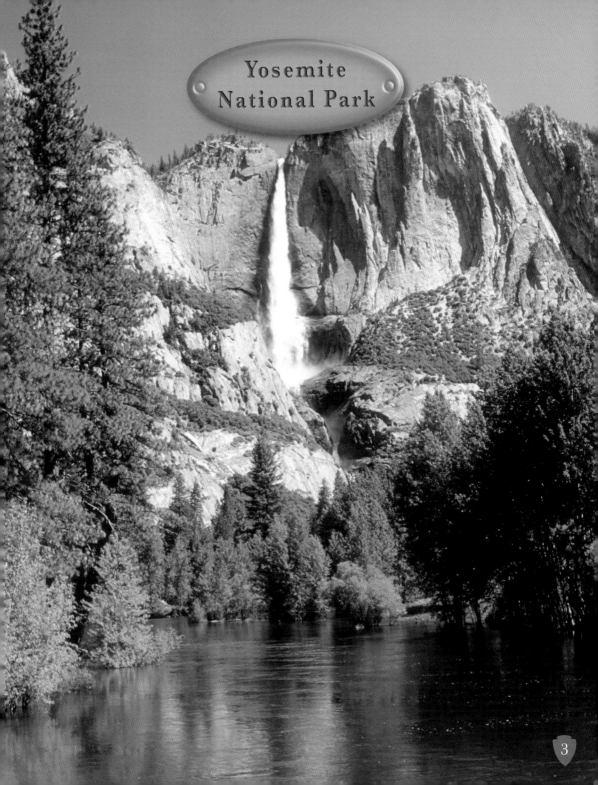

Yosemite
National Park

Why were the national parks created?

In 1870 a group of explorers spent time in an area of the United States called Yellowstone. They enjoyed its beautiful rivers, canyons, forests, mountains, and **geysers**. Sitting around the campfire one night, they came up with the idea of making the area a park that all Americans could enjoy. They wanted to keep its natural beauty from being changed.

The United States government agreed, and in 1872 it named Yellowstone as the first national park of the United States. Since then, all national parks have rules to protect the land, animals, and plants. Visitors to the national parks must obey the rules.

National Park Trivia

Who was president of the United States when the first national park was created?

Ulysses S. Grant

4

A geyser needs water, heat, and pressure to work. Hot rocks underground heat up the water. Hot water and steam spray upward through cracks in the earth. Boiling water and steam burst out of the geyser vent!

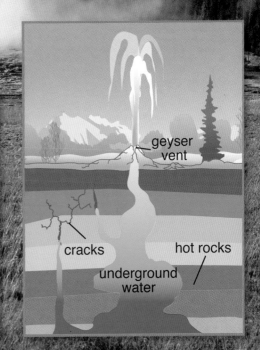

geyser vent

cracks

hot rocks

underground water

Are all national parks the same?

Our national parks are actually very different! The United States is a big country with many cultures, landforms, climates, and **ecosystems**, and our parks represent all of those things. There are 388 areas that are cared for by the National Park Service, but only 52 are called national parks. These national parks protect natural wonders like the volcanoes in Hawaii and the coral reef in the ocean at Biscayne National Park in Florida. All around the country there are parks with lakes, mountains, rivers, oceans, deserts, caves, and even sand dunes! You could say that the United States has a park for almost every kind of nature.

Biscayne
National Park

Alaska is a big state, and it has many national parks. Mountains, active and inactive volcanoes, earthquakes, **glaciers**, and some of the most dazzling landscapes in the world can be found in Alaskan national parks. These parks also have incredible animals like bears, mountain goats, moose, whales, seals, and eagles.

The Wrangell-St. Elias National Park in southern Alaska is the biggest national park in the U.S. Six Yellowstone National Parks could fit inside of it! Two Alaskan National Parks are located above the Arctic Circle and can get snow in the summer! Other Alaskan parks include Denali, Glacier Bay, Katmai, Kenai Fjords, Kobuk, and Lake Clark National Park.

National Park Trivia

How many national parks does Alaska have?

8

Which state has the most national parks?

Alaska

Saint Elias National Park

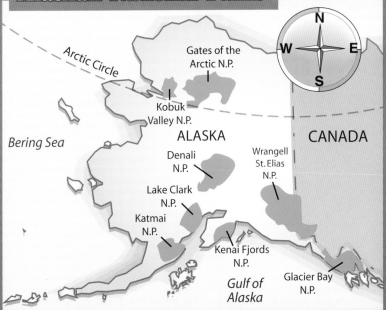

Alaskan National Parks

Arctic Circle

Gates of the Arctic N.P.

N
W — E
S

Kobuk Valley N.P.

ALASKA

CANADA

Bering Sea

Denali N.P.

Wrangell St. Elias N.P.

Lake Clark N.P.

Katmai N.P.

Kenai Fjords N.P.

Glacier Bay N.P.

Gulf of Alaska

Death Valley National Park in California is one of the hottest places on Earth. In the summer, the temperature is often well above 100 degrees Fahrenheit (F). On July 10, 1913, it was 134 degrees F in Death Valley. This is the highest temperature ever recorded in the United States. Death Valley is also the driest place in North America, with less than 2 inches of rain per year.

Amazingly, there is a lot of life in Death Valley. More than one thousand kinds of flowering and nonflowering plants live there. Some have roots that reach down 50 feet to collect water. Others have small leaves and stems that do not let water escape. At night the temperature in Death Valley drops. This is when many small animals come out of their holes to hunt.

Death Valley
National Park

Denali National Park in Alaska has the highest mountain peak in North America. Mt. McKinley is 20,320 feet high and was named for President William McKinley. However most Alaskans call this mountain peak Denali.

In 1915 Rocky Mountain National Park was created. Located in Colorado, it has 60 peaks that are over 12,000 feet high. The tallest is Longs Peak. It is 14,259 feet high. That's as tall as 11 Empire State Buildings!

Shenandoah National Park was created in 1935 and contains 300 square miles of the Blue Ridge Mountains. Located in northern Virginia, it has 2 mountain peaks that exceed 4,000 feet. These mountains are older than Denali or Longs Peak. That's why they are smaller.

Denali National Park

Rocky Mountain National Park

Shenandoah National Park

Which park is underground?

Much of Carlsbad Caverns National Park in New Mexico is underground. Carlsbad is one of the biggest series of caves in the world. Inside the caves are beautiful rock formations. In some places, the walls of the caves look like curtains. In other places, long, thin **stalactites** hang from the ceiling, and **stalagmites** rise from the floor.

Carlsbad is also famous for the Mexican free-tailed bats that live in the caves in the summer. Each night during the summer, visitors can watch over one million bats leave their caves to hunt for food.

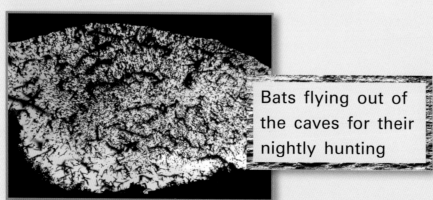

Bats flying out of the caves for their nightly hunting

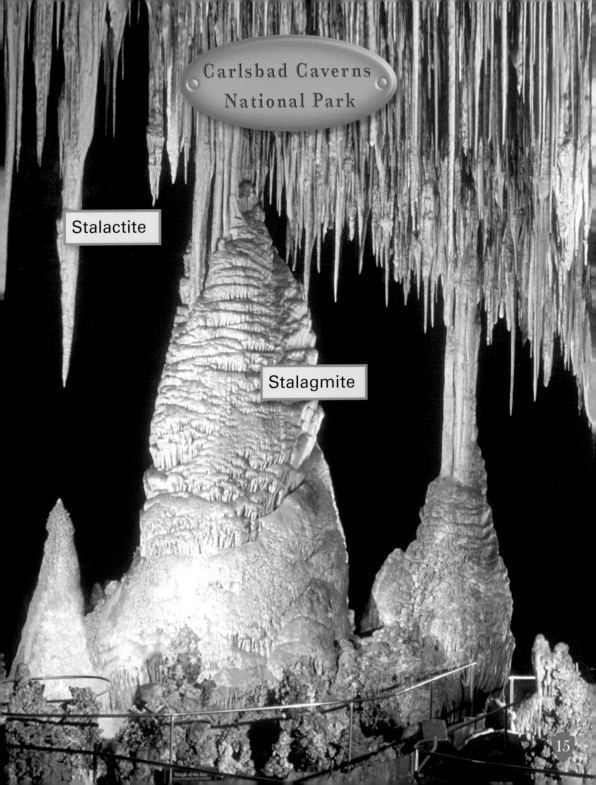

Carlsbad Caverns National Park

Stalactite

Stalagmite

What other landscapes can be found in our national parks?

Grand Canyon National Park in Arizona is one of the biggest canyons in the world. It was carved by the moving water of the Colorado River. It is huge, colorful, and unlike any other place on Earth.

Sequoia National Park in California is a forest that has some of the biggest, oldest trees in the world. The General Sherman Tree is 272 feet tall with a 36-foot wide trunk. It may be as old as 4,000 years!

The Grand Canyon from space

Sequoia
National Park

The General Sherman Tree is one of the biggest living things in the world!

Which park is full of swamps?

Crater Lake National Park in Oregon is a huge lake at the top of a mountain. The lake sits in the crater of an inactive volcano, and cliffs rise high above it.

Petrified Forest National Park in Arizona is beautiful, but it looks more like a desert than a forest! A petrified forest is a forest of trees from long ago that have turned into stone. There are no living trees in a petrified forest.

In southern Florida, Everglades National Park is full of swamps, grassy rivers, jungle islands, and rare birds.

A swamp in Everglades National Park

Crater Lake
National Park

What kinds of animals are in our national parks?

National parks are full of animals. Sea lions and elephant seals **inhabit** Channel Islands National Park in southern California. Hawaii Volcanoes National Park has many kinds of birds that are only found in Hawaii.

Some parks are great places to see the fossils of **extinct** animals. Dinosaur National Monument in Utah and Colorado has lots of dinosaur bones!

National Park Trivia

What is the only place in the world where alligators and crocodiles live together?

Everglades National Park

Alligators and Crocodiles: What's the difference?

	alligator	crocodile
snout	broad	narrow
teeth	when mouth is closed, only the upper teeth show	when mouth is closed, the upper and lower teeth show

Channel Islands
National Park

Which park would you like to visit?

Every year millions of people visit national parks. Every park is different, so each offers different activities. Canoeing is popular in the grassy waters of the Everglades. **Spelunking**, or cave exploring, is popular in Carlsbad Caverns. Serious rock climbers go to Yosemite National Park in California. In some of the Alaskan national parks, people climb glaciers or travel with dog sleds! Almost all of the national parks are great for hiking, climbing, and taking pictures.

Whether you want to climb the highest mountain in North America, swim near a coral reef, or just sit and look at pretty scenery, there is definitely a national park for you!

Glossary

ecosystems communities of living things and their environments

extinct no longer existing

geysers cracks in the earth where hot water and steam spray upward

glaciers huge masses of ice that move slowly

inhabit live in

spelunking exploring caves

stalactites rock-like structures that hang from the roof of a cave. They look like icicles.

stalagmites rock-like structures that form on the floor of a cave. They look like upside down icicles.

Index

24